Jam Session

Michael Jordan

Denis Dougherty
ABDO Publishing Company

Published by ABDO Publishing Company, 4940 Viking Drive, Suite 622, Edina, Minnesota 55435.
Copyright © 1999 by Abdo Consulting Group, Inc. International copyrights reserved in all countries.
No part of this book may be reproduced in any form without written permission from the publisher.

Published 1999
Printed in the United States of America
Second Printing 2002

Cover and Interior Photo credits: AP/Wide World Photos

Edited by Terri Dougherty

Sources: Chicago Sun Times; NBA Inside Stuff; New York Times; Sports Illustrated;
Sports Illustrated For Kids; The Sporting News; USA Today

Library of Congress Cataloging-in-Publication Data

Dougherty, Denis, 1963-
    Michael Jordan / Denis Dougherty.
        p.   cm. -- (Jam Session)
    Includes index.
    Summary: A biography of the multi-talented basketball star for the Chicago Bulls, who has won
    ten NBA scoring titles and been named NBA's Defensive Player of the Year.
    ISBN 1-57765-038-7 (hardcover)
    ISBN 1-57765-340-8 (paperback)
    1. Jordan, Michael, 1963-   --Juvenile literature. 2. Basketball players--United States--
    Biography--Juvenile literature. 3. Chicago Bulls (Basketball team)--Juvenile literature.
    [1. Jordan, Michael, 1963- .2. Basketball players. 3. Afro-Americans--Biography.]
    I. Title. II. Series.
    GV884.J67D68   1999
    796.323'092
    [B]--DC21

                                                                        98-22325
                                                                          CIP
                                                                          AC

Contents

The Best Ever 4

Humble Beginnings 6

Nothing Could Be Finer 8

Turning Pro 12

Bouncing Back 14

Help From the Supporting Cast 16

A Champion at Last 18

Staying on Top 20

Batter Up 22

Back Where He Belongs 24

Jordan Profile 27

Chronology 28

Glossary 31

Index 32

The Best Ever

When sports fans discuss the greatest players of all time there are always some arguments.

In football, simply discussing quarterbacks brings up John Elway, Dan Marino, Joe Montana, Terry Bradshaw, and Johnny Unitas. In baseball, just talking about center fielders breaks fans into groups supporting Joe DiMaggio, Willie Mays, Mickey Mantle, and Ken Griffey, Jr.

But in basketball there is little argument regarding who is the greatest player ever. That honor belongs to the Chicago Bulls' extraordinary Michael Jordan.

Early in Michael's career he was compared to the Los Angeles Lakers' Magic Johnson and the Boston Celtics' Larry Bird. But by the early 1990s there was no longer any comparison.

"Michael is the best," Magic said after the Bulls defeated the Lakers to win the 1991 NBA title. Bird commented, "It's a great honor just to be compared to Michael Jordan." Soaring through the air, Michael

Michael tips in a rebound over Utah's John Stockton during Game 2 of the 1998 NBA Finals.

thrills fans with gravity-defying moves to the basket. He jumps so high some people call him Superman. Always hustling on defense, he's just as feared on the opposite end of the court.

Michael's ability to dominate on offense and defense sets him apart. He has the highest career scoring average in pro basketball history. He has won 10 scoring titles and five Most Valuable Player (MVP) awards. Michael also has been named to the NBA All-Defensive First Team nine times, and was selected the NBA's Defensive Player of the Year in 1988. He has led the Bulls to six NBA titles in the 1990s. Michael loves competition and doing what no one else can do. His enormous physical talent is matched only by his mental approach to the game. He is an extremely smart player. He has an outstanding work ethic that has helped him improve from an average outside shooter to the best point-producer professional basketball has ever seen.

Michael drives past Shandon Anderson in Game 4 of the 1998 NBA Finals.

Humble Beginnings

Michael Jordan's road to stardom included some bumps. But Michael's desire to succeed overcame any disappointments that stood between himself and the top.

On February 17, 1963, Michael was born in Brooklyn, New York. His father, James, was attending a training program there. The family soon returned home to Wallace, North Carolina.

In 1970, the family moved to Wilmington, North Carolina, where Michael grew up with two brothers and two sisters. They often played sports together. He and his older brother, Larry, wore down the grass in their backyard playing basketball.

Larry didn't take it easy on Michael during their basketball games. He was taller than Michael and routinely won, but that made Michael determined to keep trying.

Michael also enjoyed baseball. He pitched two no-hitters in Little League and his team won a championship.

Michael grew to be lean and lanky. His ears stuck out, and some kids made fun of the way he stuck out his tongue when he was concentrating on a shot. He didn't even realize he was doing it— he was unconsciously imitating his father, who stuck out his tongue when he was concentrating on a hard job.

When Michael was a sophomore at Laney High School, he hoped to make the varsity basketball team. But when he saw the list of players on the team, his name wasn't on it. He was very disappointed but determined to become a better player.

Being on the junior varsity team gave Michael time to improve and to grow. He was 5-foot-10 when he was cut, but he was 6-foot-2 when he made the varsity team. He was taller than anyone in his family.

During high school Michael was invited to a summer basketball camp. He won many trophies at the camp and began attracting the interest of college recruiters.

People knew Michael was a good player, but no one saw him as the superstar he would become. He wasn't even on the list of the nation's top 300 college prospects!

"He had real long arms and big hands, and you could tell he was probably a good player," his high school assistant coach, Fred Lynch, once said. "But nothing about him jumped out at you."

As a young player, Michael (L) practiced many hours to perfect his game.

Nothing Could Be Finer

Growing up, Michael was a North Carolina State fan. But after visiting Chapel Hill, he chose rival North Carolina and legendary coach Dean Smith for his college career.

When Michael joined the North Carolina basketball team in the fall of 1981, he wasn't the star. The Tar Heels, who had reached the NCAA Tournament finals in 1981 only to lose to Indiana, included All-Americans James Worthy and Sam Perkins. Jimmy Black and Matt Doherty were also penciled in as starters.

Michael Jordan in the 1984 NCAA Tournament.

Michael was not yet a great shooter, but his defense and athletic ability made him a contender for the last starting spot. Coach Smith didn't announce the fifth starter until he posted the lineup on the bulletin board before the season opener. Michael Jordan saw his name! He would be only the fourth freshman ever to start for North Carolina.

The Tar Heels were ranked No. 1 in the country

for most of the 1981-82 season. There was pressure on the team to bring Smith his first national title. Smith's teams had lost in the NCAA finals in 1968, 1977, and 1981.

The Tar Heels won the Atlantic Coast Conference regular season and tournament titles. In the tournament final, Michael made four clutch jump shots late in the game. The Heels beat Virginia and 7-foot-4 center Ralph Sampson, 47-45.

The Tar Heels rolled to the national championship game in New Orleans. But there, blocking North Carolina's path to the title, was Georgetown and its intimidating 7-foot freshman center Patrick Ewing.

Ewing had a brilliant game. But Michael got the best of Patrick when it counted.

Georgetown went ahead 62-61 with 32 seconds to go. Matt Doherty passed to Michael on the left baseline, 16 feet from the hoop.

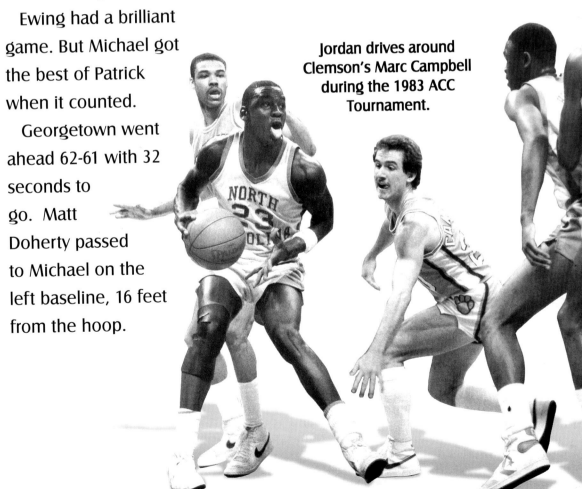

Jordan drives around Clemson's Marc Campbell during the 1983 ACC Tournament.

With 17 seconds left, the freshman calmly went up for the jump shot. SWISH!

The Tar Heels won 63-62. Thanks to Michael Jordan, Dean Smith finally had his first national title!

Michael was now famous for making "The Shot," but he didn't let the success go to his head. He led the Tar Heels to another ACC title, and to the 1983 regional final. North Carolina lost 82-77 to Georgia, despite Michael's 26 points.

Michael was a consensus All-America selection. He was also named national Player of the Year!

"There is one phenomenon in college basketball, and his name is Michael Jordan," NBA scout Tom Newell said.

An ACC rival said: "Michael Jordan is Superman."

With Michael and Sam Perkins returning, North Carolina cruised to the ACC regular season and tournament titles in the 1983-84 season. The Heels took a 27-2 record and the nation's No. 1 ranking into the East Regional.

But in the regional semifinals Michael suffered one of the biggest disappointments of his basketball career. Legendary coach Bob Knight's Indiana team stunned the Heels 72-68. Michael scored only 13 points.

The loss, however, couldn't hide the fact that Michael had a great season. He again was named college basketball's Player of the Year.

That summer, he played on the United States Olympic team coached by Knight. The team won its eight games by an average of 32 points and capped its remarkable run with a 96-65 win over

Spain in the gold-medal game in Los Angeles. Michael gave his gold medal to his mother.

The Olympic team included Ewing, Perkins, Chris Mullin, and Steve Alford. Many called it the best amateur team ever. Michael, who averaged a team-high 17.1 points per game, was the star of stars.

After one game, Spain's coach joked: "I asked my good friend Bob Knight if he wanted my whole team in a trade for Michael Jordan."

U.S.A.'s Michael Jordan is airborne as Spain's players try to stop him in the 1984 Olympics.

Turning Pro

*A*fter his junior year, Michael faced a difficult decision. He could stay at North Carolina for one more season and earn his degree. Or he could turn pro.

It was his mother's dream for him to earn a college degree. But if he stayed at North Carolina he would risk getting injured. That would hurt his chances in the NBA Draft and could cost him a lot of money.

Michael thought long and hard about his decision. He talked to his coach, his parents, and his teammates. In the end, he decided to turn pro. He promised his mother he'd finish his studies, a promise he kept. He wanted to compete at the highest level.

Michael was the third pick of the 1984 NBA Draft, behind two seven-foot centers. Houston, drafting first, took the University of Houston's Hakeem Olajuwon. Portland then took Kentucky's Sam Bowie. The Trail Blazers felt they needed a center more than they needed Michael.

The Chicago Bulls, who had never reached the NBA Finals in their 18-year history, gratefully selected Michael. They knew they had a good player, but no one knew he'd become a superstar.

"Jordan isn't going to turn this franchise around," Bulls general manager Rod Thorn said at the time.

But soon after Michael opened his rookie season on October 26, 1984, he proved he was among the NBA's top players. That season he averaged 28.2 points per game, was named to the NBA All-Star team and won the Rookie of the Year award.

However, Michael had to adjust to something North Carolina had not prepared him for: losing. While he had played with many talented teammates in a team-oriented system at North Carolina, Michael was the only go-to guy for Chicago.

The Bulls' regular season record during Michael's first season was only 38-44. With Michael aboard they made the playoffs for the first time in four years, but were eliminated in the first round by the Milwaukee Bucks.

Michael, however, had made an imprint on the team and the NBA. He stood out because of his hard work at practice and his spectacular moves on the court. Attendance at Bulls games nearly doubled during his rookie season. He was popular with the fans, and sneakers and shirts with his number 23 on them were best-sellers.

Air Jordan had arrived!

Michael signs with the Bulls on September 12, 1984.

Bouncing Back

Michael was eager to start his second season in the NBA, but in the third game of the year something happened that changed his plans. He broke a tiny bone in his foot and missed 64 games.

This was the first time in his life he had to miss a basketball game because of an injury. Sitting on the sidelines was definitely not a role Michael liked. He was very eager to play again.

In March, he convinced the team's owner he was ready to play and took to the court. As soon as he got the basketball in his hands, he took it to the hoop for a slam dunk!

The Bulls earned the last playoff spot in the Eastern Conference. They faced Boston in the first round and, while Michael was spectacular, the veteran Celtics swept the series in three games. Boston went on to win the title.

But Michael earned the respect of his opponents. He scored 49 points in one game and a playoff-record 63 in another. "I think he's God disguised as Michael Jordan," the Celtics' Bird said.

Jordan goes up for the slam.

During the 1986-87 season, Michael was a scoring machine. He averaged 37.1 points per game, the highest average ever by anyone other than Wilt Chamberlain. He won the first of seven straight NBA scoring titles and the first of two straight Slam Dunk titles. He became the only guard in NBA history to get more than 200 steals and 100 blocked shots, a feat he would repeat the next season.

Over and above his stellar statistics, Michael wowed teammates, opponents, and fans with his soaring drives and rim-rattling slam dunks. His "hang time" became legendary.

But Michael couldn't win a title by himself. The Bulls were again bounced from the playoffs by the Celtics in three games.

Jordan is known for his hang time as shown here in 1986.

Help From the Supporting Cast

*M*ichael continued to put up incredible numbers in the 1987-1988 season. He became the first player ever named the NBA's MVP and its Defensive Player of the Year for the same season.

But more importantly, the Bulls got some players who could help Jordan win a championship. Scottie Pippen and Horace Grant had been acquired in the 1987 draft.

Michael was the ultimate shooting star at the 1988 All-Star Game in Chicago. He made 17 of 23 field-goal attempts and scored 40 points to win the MVP.

After the game, Magic Johnson was asked how he ranked the best players in the league: "There's Michael, and then there's everybody else," Magic said.

There was no doubt Michael was the best individual player in the league, but there were questions about his ability to lead a team to a title. The Bulls made it past Cleveland in five games in the first round of the playoffs. Then Chicago faced a rough, tough Detroit Pistons team in the second round.

Michael had some good games, but struggled against great defensive players Joe Dumars and Dennis Rodman. Detroit's defense helped the Pistons beat the Bulls four games to one.

The Bulls had talent, but it took time for things to come together. Michael hit a clutch shot at the buzzer to win the decisive fifth game of a playoff series against Cleveland in 1989. But the Pistons eliminated the Bulls in the Eastern Conference finals in 1989 and 1990. Michael scored a career-high 69 points in a game at Cleveland in 1990, but still had an empty feeling when the season ended.

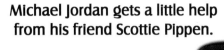

Michael Jordan gets a little help from his friend Scottie Pippen.

A Champion at Last

As the 1990-91 season began, Michael Jordan had done everything a basketball player could do—except win an NBA championship. With Michael shooting, dunking, rebounding, making steals, and blocking shots, the Bulls rolled to the best record in the East at 61-21. Michael won his second MVP, but he wanted more. He set his sights on a title.

Under coach Phil Jackson, the Bulls began doing things a bit differently. They still relied heavily on Jordan, but his teammates had more scoring responsibility.

Jordan applies the pressure on Magic Johnson in the 1991 NBA Finals.

Once again, Chicago met Detroit in the Eastern finals. This time things ended differently. Chicago pulled away from Detroit in the first game and its confidence soared. The Bulls swept the series!

Now the Bulls were ready to take on the Lakers, and the much-anticipated "Michael vs. Magic" matchup arrived. Magic Johnson had five championship rings, and Michael none, but the Bulls had home-court advantage.

Michael's teammates were nervous. The Bulls lost on their home court in the first NBA Finals game in the team's history. The Lakers' Sam Perkins, Michael's former North Carolina teammate, won the game with a three-pointer. Michael's potential game-tying shot bounced out at the buzzer. "At least, it took another Tar Heel to beat us," Michael said.

In the second game, Michael made an effort to get his teammates involved. He didn't shoot much in the first half and passed to teammates for easy baskets. The Bulls won easily. Then they won three straight games in Los Angeles. They had their first NBA title!

Michael was his usual brilliant self, taking home the Finals MVP as well as the regular-season MVP. However, it was the play of teammates Pippen, Grant, and John Paxson that made the difference.

Michael Jordan slams with authority.

Staying on Top

Michael was clearly in a class by himself in the 1991-92 season. He won his third MVP Award and led the Bulls to an NBA best 67-15 record.

In the second round of the playoffs, Chicago was tested by a new rival, the New York Knicks, led by Patrick Ewing. The Knicks stunned the Bulls by winning the first game of the series in Chicago, but the Bulls emerged on top in Game 7.

Chicago took care of Cleveland and Portland to repeat as NBA champions. Michael put on an incredible show in the first game of the Finals, scoring a Finals-record 35 points in the first half.

Michael was again Finals MVP.

That summer Michael played on the "Dream Team" that stormed to the 1992 Olympic gold medal in Barcelona, Spain.

The next season the Bulls wanted more. They wanted a "three-peat."

Michael Jordan celebrates after the Bulls win their third consecutive NBA championship.

No team had won three titles in a row since the Celtics had won eight straight from 1959-1966. Could they do it?

The Bulls cruised through the playoffs with Michael leading the way. Chicago's NBA Finals opponent was the Phoenix Suns. Chicago had a chance to win the title in the sixth game of the series. The Bulls were down by two points with a few seconds remaining. Horace Grant had the ball, and looked to pass to Michael but he was double-covered.

Instead, Grant passed to teammate John Paxson, who made a three-point shot. The

Bulls won 99-98. The "three-peat" was theirs!

Michael was just as happy with Paxson making the winning shot as he would have been making it himself. "I knew Pax would hit that shot," Michael said afterward. Jordan had averaged a Finals-record 41 points in the series and won his third straight Finals MVP!

Batter Up

After the 1993 season it seemed Michael had done it all: three NBA championships, three MVPs, two Olympic gold medals, and award after award.

He also had all that came with fame, both the good and the bad. He made millions of dollars, was adored and idolized all over the world, and had the respect of everyone in the NBA. But he had little privacy. He couldn't take his kids to Disney World without being recognized and swarmed by fans. His every move was scrutinized.

In the summer of 1993, he faced the worst. His father, James, was murdered. The tragedy hit Michael hard. His father was also his best friend. He was troubled by the loss.

Basketball became less important to Michael. Winning games couldn't bring his father back. It also couldn't give him more time with his wife, Juanita, and their three children. Michael decided to retire from basketball.

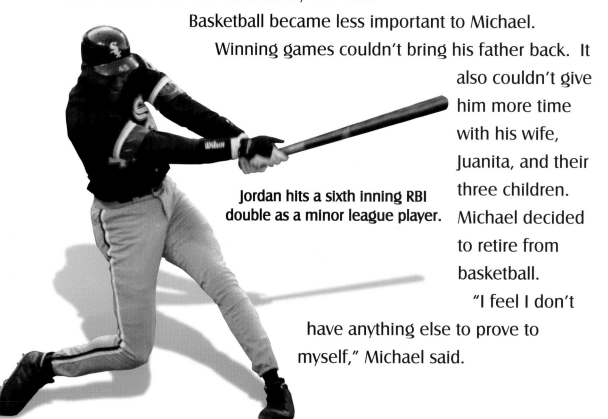

Jordan hits a sixth inning RBI double as a minor league player.

"I feel I don't have anything else to prove to myself," Michael said.

Michael left basketball at the top of his game. He was still playing like a superstar and his team was winning. But he wanted a new challenge.

Michael didn't stay retired for long. The next spring he began secretly working out with the Chicago White Sox baseball team. He had been a pitcher in high school, and was fast enough to steal bases and play the outfield.

But hitting the baseball was another matter. He tried hard and impressed his coaches and teammates by applying the same dedication to baseball as he had to basketball.

Michael played for a White Sox minor-league team, the Class AA Birmingham Barons of the Southern League. He had a lot of trouble hitting the ball. It didn't look like he would be good enough to make it to the major leagues, but he didn't quit. He finished the season hitting .202, with 30 stolen bases, and was in spring training the next February.

But baseball was in turmoil. The major-league players were on strike. Michael could have played in the majors as a replacement player for those on strike, but he didn't think that was right. Michael decided to leave the game and go back to his true love: basketball.

Outfielder Michael Jordan goes after a fly ball.

Back Where He Belongs

Soon the word was out. Michael would return to the Bulls in time for another run at a title. Amid much fanfare, Michael returned to basketball in a game at Indiana. He made only one basket in the first half. He finished with 19 points, and was exhausted after the 103-96 overtime loss.

But he soon showed some of the flair of the Michael of old, scoring 55 points in a game against the Knicks. He led the Bulls, a team that had struggled to be above .500 without him, to a 13-4 record the rest of the way.

Under Michael's leadership, the Bulls beat the Charlotte Hornets in the first round of the playoffs. Then they faced the Orlando Magic and lost in six games.

In the off-season, Michael worked as hard as he ever had at improving his game. In the 1995-96 season, he led the Bulls to the best record in NBA history at 72-10 and won his fourth MVP Award.

"I feel my game is where it was two years ago," Jordan said early in the season. "I'm real pumped about this season and about my contribution to the team."

The Bulls beat Seattle in six games for the NBA title. Michael won his fourth Finals MVP. The next season, Chicago won 69 games. Utah's Karl Malone edged Michael for the MVP, but Michael got his revenge in the NBA Finals.

Michael had always played his best in pressure situations, and he showed it in the first game. With the score tied, Michael faded to his left and launched a 21-foot jump shot over the Jazz's Bryon

Russell with less than a second left in the game. The ball hit nothing but net. The fans at Chicago's United Center cheered wildly as Michael raised his fist in triumph.

With the series tied 2-2, Michael came down with an awful stomach virus before Game 5. He felt terrible, but he knew the team needed him.

"Sometimes you've got to come out and do what you've got to do," Michael said. "As a leader, I had to do my best."

Michael scored 38 points, including a huge three-point shot with 25 seconds left, and grabbed seven rebounds. All this while he was so sick he almost passed out in the third quarter. The Bulls won 90-88.

Shandon Anderson, of the Utah Jazz, tries to guard Michael in the 1998 NBA Finals.

In Game 6, they racked up another title. The Bulls had their fifth title of the '90s. Michael scored 39 points and took home his fifth Finals MVP.

The following season, Jordan led his Bulls back to the NBA Finals for a shot at a "repeat of the three-peat." Once again the Bulls were matched against the Utah Jazz and the results were much the same. In the sixth game, the Bulls grabbed their sixth title in eight seasons.

With Scottie Pippen sitting out part of the sixth game with back spasms, Michael worked his magic, scoring a game-high 45 points and winning his sixth Finals MVP.

Jordan goes for the dunk against the Utah Jazz during the 1998 NBA Finals.

His 44th and 45th points were the most dramatic. Down one, Michael stole the ball, dribbled, slithered around to shake off Utah's Bryon Russell, and shot a jumper from near the top of the key with 5.2 seconds left to give Chicago a stunning 87-86 victory.

As NBA Commissioner David Stern said: "Time and again, he shows us he's the best basketball player in the world."

Jordan Profile

Height: 6 feet, 6 inches
Born: Feb. 17, 1963, in Brooklyn, N.Y.
Home: Highland Park, Ill.
College: University of North Carolina
Pro Teams: Chicago Bulls 1984-1993, 1995-present
     Birmingham Barons 1994
NBA MVP award winner: 1988, 1991, 1992, 1996, 1998
NBA championships and Finals MVP: 1991, 1992, 1993, 1996, 1997, 1998
Personal: Always wears his University of North Carolina shorts under his Bulls uniform for good luck ... Starred in first major motion picture "Space Jam" in 1996 ... Very active in supporting the James R. Jordan Boys & Girls Club charity ... Enjoys pregame meal of steak and eggs ... Favorite road arena is Madison Square Garden in New York ... Favorite subject in school was math ... Has one dog, an Akita ... He and his wife, Juanita, have three children, Jeffrey, Marcus, and Jasmine.

Honors

NBA Finals MVP: 1991, 1992, 1993, 1996, 1997, 1998
NBA MVP: 1988, 1991, 1992, 1996, 1998
All-NBA First Team: 1987, 1988, 1989, 1990, 1991, 1992, 1993, 1996, 1997, 1998
NBA Defensive Player of the Year: 1988
NBA All-Defensive First Team: 1988, 1989, 1990, 1991, 1992, 1993, 1996, 1997, 1998
All-Star Game starter: 1985 to 1993 and 1996 to 1998
NBA All-Star Game MVP: 1988, 1996, 1998
NBA Rookie of the Year: 1985
Slam Dunk champion: 1987 and 1988

Records

Highest career regular-season scoring average (31.7)
Most seasons leading league in scoring (10)
Most seasons with 2,000 or more points (11)
Highest career playoff scoring average (33.6)
Most points in a playoff game (63, vs. Boston, April 20, 1986)
Most points in the first half of an NBA Finals game (35, vs. Portland, June 3, 1992)
Highest scoring average in an NBA Finals (41.0, vs. Phoenix, 1993)
Only guard to record more than 200 steals and 100 blocks in a season
Consecutive points scored by one player on a team (23, vs. Atlanta, April 16, 1987)
Most free throws made in one half (20, vs. Miami, Dec. 30, 1992)
Most free throws attempted in one half (23, vs. Miami, Dec. 30, 1992)

Chronology

1963 - Born on Feb. 17 in Brooklyn, New York.

1981 - Graduated from Laney High School in Wilmington, North Carolina. Began college career at the University of North Carolina.

1982 - As a freshman, hits "The Shot" as North Carolina beats Georgetown to win the NCAA championship.

1983 - Named College Player of the Year.

   - Unanimous selection for First Team All-America.

1984 - Named College Player of the Year.

   - Wins the Dr. James Naismith Award.

   - Leaves college early and enters the NBA Draft. Chosen by the Chicago Bulls with the third pick of the draft.

   - Wins a gold medal as a member of the U.S. Olympic basketball team, coached by Bob Knight.

1985 - NBA Rookie of the Year.

   - Named to the NBA All-Rookie team.

   - Starts NBA All-Star Game.

1986 - Sets NBA playoff record for most points in a game with 63 in Boston.

1987 - Named to the All-NBA First Team.

   - NBA All-Star Game starter.

   - Leads league in scoring with career-high 37.1-point average.

   - Records more than 200 steals and 100 blocks in a season, only guard in NBA history to do so.

   - Wins NBA Slam Dunk competition.

1988 - NBA Most Valuable Player.
   - NBA Defensive Player of the Year
   - Sets NBA record for a guard with 131 blocks.
   - Leads NBA in steals.
   - NBA All-Star Game MVP.
   - Wins NBA Slam Dunk competition.
   - Named to the All-NBA First Team.
   - Named to NBA All-Defensive First Team.
   - NBA All-Star Game starter.
   - NBA scoring leader.
1989 - Marries Juanita Vanoy on Sept. 2.
   - Named to the All-NBA First Team.
   - NBA scoring leader.
   - Named to NBA All-Defensive First Team.
1990 - Scores career-high 69 points at Cleveland
   - Leads NBA in steals
   - NBA scoring leader.
1991 - Bulls are NBA champions for first time.
   - NBA MVP.
   - NBA Finals MVP.
   - NBA scoring leader.
1992 - Bulls repeat as NBA champions.
   - Member of gold-medal winning U.S. Olympic basketball team.
   - NBA MVP.
   - NBA Finals MVP.
   - NBA scoring leader.

1993 - Bulls "three-peat" as NBA champions.
- Leads NBA in steals.
- NBA Finals MVP.
- NBA scoring leader.
- Retires from basketball on October 6.

1994 - Becomes a professional baseball player. Spends 1994 season with the Birmingham Barons, a Class AA minor-league team.
- Has .202 batting average, three home runs, 51 RBIs, 30 stolen bases.

1995 - Returns to basketball on March 18.

1996 - Bulls are NBA champions.
- NBA Finals MVP.
- NBA MVP.
- NBA All-Star Game MVP.
- NBA scoring leader.

1997 - Bulls are NBA champions.
- NBA Finals MVP.
- NBA scoring leader.

1998 - Bulls "repeat the three-peat" as NBA champions.
- NBA Finals MVP.
- NBA MVP.
- NBA All-Star Game MVP.
- NBA scoring leader.

Glossary

CONFERENCE - A group of college or professional athletic teams.

FIELD GOAL - A basket worth two or three points.

FRESHMAN - A student in the first year of high school or college in the United States.

HANG TIME - Amount of time spent in the air before making a shot.

JUNIOR - A student in the third year of high school or college in the United States.

NATIONAL BASKETBALL ASSOCIATION (NBA) - A group of teams competing at the highest level of professional basketball.

PLAYOFFS - Games played after the regular season to determine the champion.

SOPHOMORE - A student in the second year of high school or college in the United States.

SPRING TRAINING - Practices and games played in the spring months before the regular baseball season begins.

STATISTICS - Numbers used to present information about a player's ability.

THREE-PEAT - To win three championships in a row.

VARSITY - The main team representing a school in sports or other activities.

Index

A

Air Jordan 13
Alford, Steve 11
All-Defensive First Team
  5, 27, 29
All-Star Game 16, 27, 28,
  29, 30

B

Barcelona, Spain 20
baseball 4, 6, 23, 30
Bird, Larry 4, 14
Birmingham Barons 23, 27,
  30
Black, Jimmy 8
Boston Celtics 4, 14, 27,
  28
Bowie, Sam 12
Bradshaw, Terry 4
Brooklyn, New York 6, 28

C

Chamberlain, Wilt 15
Chapel Hill 8
Charlotte Hornets 24
Chicago Bulls 4, 12, 27, 28
Chicago White Sox 23

D

Defensive Player of the Year
  16, 27, 29
Detroit Pistons 16
DiMaggio, Joe 4
Doherty, Matt 8, 10
Dumars, Joe 16

E

Eastern Conference 14, 17
Elway, John 4
Ewing, Patrick 9, 20

G

Georgetown 9, 10, 28
Grant, Horace 16, 21
Griffey Jr., Ken 4

I

Indiana Pacers 8, 10, 24
injury 14

J

Jackson, Phil 18
Johnson, Magic 4, 16, 18

K

Knight, Bob 10, 11, 28

L

Laney High School 6, 28
Los Angeles Lakers 4, 11,
  18, 19

M

Malone, Karl 24
Mantle, Mickey 4
Marino, Dan 4
Mays, Willie 4
Milwaukee Bucks 13
Montana, Joe 4
Mullin, Chris 11
MVP 5, 16, 18, 19, 20, 21,
  22, 24, 26, 27, 29, 30

N

NBA Draft 12, 28
NCAA Tournament 8
New York Knicks 20
Newell, Tom 10
North Carolina 6, 8, 9, 10,
  12, 13, 19, 27, 28

O

Olajuwon, Hakeem 12
Orlando Magic 24

P

Paxson, John 19, 21
Perkins, Sam 8, 10, 19
Phoenix Suns 21
Pippen, Scottie 16, 17, 26
Player of the Year 5, 10, 16,
  27, 28, 29
Portland Trail Blazers 12

R

Rodman, Dennis 16
Rookie of the Year 13, 27,
  28
Russell, Bryon 24, 25, 26

S

Sampson, Ralph 9
Slam Dunk title 15

T

Tar Heels 8, 9, 10

U

Unitas, Johnny 4
United Center 25
United States Olympic team
  11

W

Worthy, James 8

92   Dougherty, Denis
JOR   Michael Jordan

JUN   2009

DATE DUE

JUL 0 1 2009
.JUL 2 7 2009
AUG 1 1 2009
FEB 2 3 2010